© **Ringpress Books**
PO Box 8, Lydney,
Gloucestershire, GL15 4YN
United Kingdom.
Tel: 01594 845577
Fax: 01594 845599
e-mail:
ringpress@petbookshop.com

ISBN 1 86054 176 3

Fists published 1999
All rights reserved.

PHOTOGRAPHS:
Amanda Bulbeck.
DESIGN:
Rob Benson

ALL ABOUT
TRAINING
YOUR DOG

Alison Hornsby

Contents

Owning a well-trained dog, one that is welcome everywhere you go, is something to be proud of. However, a dog cannot teach himself. He is dependent on his owner not only for love and care, but also for encouragement and direction to shape his behaviour.

Bad habits are easily established and soon become an everyday occurrence. A bad habit is usually a way of behaving that has not been controlled – and before long, you end up with a dog that is blamed for his undesirable, anti-social behaviour.

If you decide to own a dog, you must be prepared to take on the task of training, which is a process that continues throughout a dog's life.

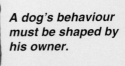

A dog's behaviour must be shaped by his owner.

Before You Start

Think carefully before making your choice. If you opt for a pedigree (pure-bred) dog, find out as much as possible about the breed's traits and characteristics. Too many people purchase a dog because they have admired a friend's

Consider how much time you can give to training your dog.

well-behaved pet, or they have seen a particular breed competing in Obedience, Agility, or Sheepdog Trials, little realising how much effort has gone into achieving the end result.

If you decide on a cross-breed, or an adult dog from a rescue shelter, it is more difficult to predict how your dog will turn out. Mixed parentage can produce a wonderful dog, but you can only make a guess when it comes to assessing adult size and character. The rescued dog may have experienced trauma in his early life, and therefore expert handling and training could be required.

Obedience Champions make it all look easy, but never under-estimate the effort that has gone into achieving this level of success.

First and foremost try to 'think dog', and avoid attributing human feelings or emotions to your pet. Your dog will see you as another dog and will react accordingly.

The dog is a social animal; he enjoys company, especially group activities such as playing and hunting. He needs and enjoys physical contact through touch, grooming and cuddles.

Dogs communicate through body postures and facial expressions. This 'language' can be used as a basis for training and understanding canine behaviour.

Your dog will be happier if you make your desires clear and establish household rules that he respects and adheres to. There is no need to shout or bully to achieve good results. Training is a continuous learning process which takes time and patience.

Learn how to 'think dog'.

Key Points

•Training should be an enjoyable experience for you and your dog.

•Sessions should be short. Little and often is the best approach.

•Learn to read your dog's facial expressions and body posture, and this will help you to interpret his attitude or intentions in different situations.

•If you reward good behaviour, there is a good chance it will be repeated.

•Ignore unacceptable behaviour, and it is likely to decrease.

Understand your dog by observing body posture and facial expression.

Special Needs

If you have chosen an adult dog from a rescue centre, or have rehomed a dog through a breed rescue organisation, the dog will probably have some established routines and behaviour patterns which may take time to reveal themselves. With time, understanding, and some re-directional training, the outcome can still be extremely rewarding.

A dog from a rescue shelter will need special consideration.

The Right Start

House Rules

It is important to be consistent with your dog. All members of the household should be encouraged to adopt the same attitude and approach. Decide beforehand on the standard of behaviour you wish to achieve from your dog and what you will, and will not, allow.

All families have their own 'rules', but unacceptable habits usually include: jumping up, mouthing/biting, excessive barking, stealing, begging from the table, or letting your dog climb on furniture.

The dog is a pack animal. It is important for your dog that you adopt the role of leader, and make the rules as clear as possible. A dog that is allowed to take control will behave like a spoilt child. He will demand to be the centre of attention at all times, and he will soon become a nuisance.

Early Learning

Obedience is the basis of all dog training. Dogs are usually quick to learn their name and the command "No". The next stage is to start work on the essential exercises which should include: Heel, Sit, Down and Come.

Keep training sessions short (five to ten minutes at a time), and teach one command at a time. This will avoid any confusion in your dog's mind. Good behaviour should be rewarded with a food treat, a game with a favourite toy, or giving physical or verbal praise.

The Right Tone

Effective use of your voice, and accurate timing of commands and praise, will help your dog to learn quickly. Error-free learning is the key to success.

Listen to your voice. Does it sound cheerful and genuine? Remember, training should be fun for both you and your puppy.

Practise getting the tone right. Women find the deeper, stern voice of disapproval difficult to achieve. Men, on the other hand, find the lighter, more encouraging, tone needed for praise more difficult or embarrassing.

The first rule of dog training is: do not be self-conscious! Inhibited body language or a subdued tone of voice means a block in communication and understanding.

The Right Start

Bad Habits

A mistake often made by first-time dog owners is the expectation that as a puppy matures he will stop behaving badly. In reality, bad behaviour becomes an established pattern which becomes increasingly difficult to break.

A puppy uses his mouth to investigate new things, and this can lead to excessive mouthing or biting. Right from the start, discourage your puppy if he bites your hands or clothes. The best plan is to offer a substitute – a favourite toy – and this will distract him from further biting. Make sure you and your family always follow this procedure, and encourage visitors to do the same.

The natural instincts demonstrated by some breeds can develop into unacceptable behaviour. For example, the herding breeds (particularly Border Collies) will often chase traffic. Gundogs (such as Labrador Retrievers and Golden Retrievers) have a strong sense of smell, and this can lead to poor recalls. The digging and ratting tendencies of some Terrier breeds (such as the Jack Russell) may give a keen gardener a few nightmares! So try to learn as much as you can about the natural instincts of your chosen breed to avoid problems developing.

A strong sense of smell is an asset in a working dog, but it can lead to poor recalls if a pet dog is allowed to use his nose unchecked.

Collie types often have a strong chasing instinct which must be curbed.

Your puppy must be taught right from wrong, from the start. It is not necessary to shout: your dog has an acute sense of hearing, and, in most cases, he will be responsive and willing to please. Discipline should be in the form of:-

• Disapproval – using a firm, low tone of voice.
• Distraction – diverting your dog's attention.
• Control – attaching the collar and lead/long line (see page 20).
• Indifference – deny your puppy attention while he is displaying unacceptable behaviour.

The desire to dig in breeds like the Jack Russell, can cause havoc in your garden.

Socialisation

Τhe importance of early socialisation is widely recognised as a formative factor in developing a sound temperament. In fact, it is often lack of socialisation which is the cause of behavioural problems seen in some adult dogs rehomed from rescue shelters.

A new puppy needs time to settle into his new home, and to get used to the sights and sounds of everyday living.

Broadening Horizons

As your puppy finds his feet, start to broaden his horizons. Make regular short journeys in the car to visit friends and relatives. Carry your puppy around the block or to the local shop. This will give him the opportunity to see and hear traffic and meet larger groups of adults and children, even though he may not have completed his inoculation programme.

Gradually introduce your puppy to busier conditions. Most puppies take everything in their stride, enjoying their outings, meeting people and, inevitably, receiving lots of attention.

If your puppy lacks confidence, slow down! Don't let him be intimidated by crowds

Broaden your puppy's horizons by introducing a variety of different experiences.

of people or noisy traffic conditions. Keep to quieter areas for longer, and then slowly introduce him to the busier areas. Puppies can easily be frightened by experiencing too much too soon. This applies equally to the adult dog who has been rehomed. Take things slowly, and give the dog time to develop his confidence and his trust in you.

As the puppy gains experience, introduce him to other conditions, such as steps, bus stations, railway stations, lifts, slippery floors and swing doors. Vary the areas you walk your puppy. Go to different parks and shops; all these activities will help with the temperamental development of your dog.

Other Dogs

It is important that your puppy learns how to mix with other dogs. The best way of doing this is by attending a local puppy class. This will provide the opportunity to teach your puppy to behave in the company of other dogs. A rescued dog will also benefit from this type of socialisation, but you will need to attend a class for adult dogs.

If you already have an older dog at home, do not allow the puppy to pester him continually. Although some adults will enjoy or tolerate a brief spell of play with the puppy, many will quickly tire of rough puppy behaviour and will end the session by putting the puppy firmly in his place.

Learning to mix with other dogs is an essential part of growing up.

Toys And Games

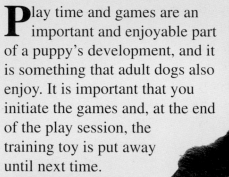

Play time and games are an important and enjoyable part of a puppy's development, and it is something that adult dogs also enjoy. It is important that you initiate the games and, at the end of the play session, the training toy is put away until next time.

Do not allow your dog to become possessive about toys.

You can teach your dog to give up a toy by offering a treat. As the dog spits the toy out, say "Give", pick up the toy and then give the treat. Reward with a stroke and verbal praise. Be consistent, and make sure you always give the command so that the response is automatic. Never allow your dog to snatch a toy from the handler.

Teach your dog to give up his toy by exchanging it for a treat.

Playing With Children

Children and dogs can develop wonderful relationships, but it is essential that both puppy and child grow up respecting one another. Children should avoid playing games of strength, such as tug-of-war and wrestling, unless they are able to control the situation.

Your puppy should not be allowed to play until he is exhausted. Energetic, enthusiastic children can easily over-excite a puppy, resulting in rough play. The puppy will play with your child in exactly the same way he would play with another dog. This means using sharp claws and needle-sharp teeth – and, inevitably, the game ends in tears. The puppy has been allowed to become excitable and boisterous, and no puppy benefits from this type of encouragement.

Children should be taught the following rules:

• Leave the puppy alone when he is in his bed.
It is important for the puppy to have plenty of opportunity to rest and sleep without being disturbed. His bed should be a place of sanctuary. If the puppy is constantly disturbed, he may become anxious and could show signs of irritability.

• Do not touch the puppy or interfere with his food bowl while he is eating.
The puppy could perceive any erratic behaviour on the part of a child as a threat. This could lead to the puppy becoming over-protective of his food or his bowl.

• Do not pick up the puppy or carry him.
Children and adults should sit on the floor, before allowing the puppy on to their lap for a cuddle. This will prevent accidents, and the puppy will learn that he cannot jump up and demand your attention ad-lib.

Children and dogs must learn mutual respect.

13

The Collar And Lead

The lead is an important training aid in all situations. It can be used around the home and garden as well as for walking out. Put your dog on the lead for all early learning sessions as this will ensure a more successful lesson. Your close proximity will give the dog confidence, you will be in control of the situation, and your dog will not be able to evade training interaction. Choose a lightweight collar and lead for this purpose.

First Steps

The best way to introduce your dog to the collar is to put it on him for short periods during play-time or while he is eating. Gradually extend the length of time you leave the collar on, over a period of two to three days. In most cases, the dog will scratch and complain for about five minutes, and will then give in and forget it is there.

Once your dog has accepted wearing a collar, condition him

to accept the lead by clipping it on for five to ten minutes and allowing it to trail. This should only be done during a supervised play session to ensure the lead does not get caught on anything.

Occasionally pick up the lead and encourage the dog towards you, using plenty of encouragement and praise. Repeat the exercise two or three times each session. Practise this procedure in the garden, as well as around the house, before venturing out on to the streets.

Lots of encouragement is needed in the early stages of lead-training.

First Walks And Exercise

Most dogs usually accept wearing the lead and collar quite quickly. They will often carry the lead in their mouth for the first few walks and frequent stops are normal.

A positive approach from the handler is required. Use plenty of verbal encouragement when the dog is actually moving. Avoid praising your dog when he stops. A sympathetic approach often encourages further reluctance.

Avoid getting too far ahead of the dog, and never be tempted to drag or pull him. Use a toy or a treat, or arrange for a friend to walk an experienced dog in front to encourage forward movement.

Walking On The Lead (Heelwork)

The aim of most pet owners is to have a dog who will walk beside them without pulling. This is how to do it.

• If your dog gets too far ahead of you, stop, call the dog's name and simultaneously jerk backwards with the lead.

• Keep facing in the direction you were travelling, and walk backwards.

• The dog will turn towards you; as he approaches, praise enthusiastically.

• Encourage the dog back into the required position on your lefthand-side, and give the command "Heel" or "Close".

• Command the dog to sit, before walking on.

The Sit

Don't forget to 'train as your dog does!' This means that any time you see your puppy moving into the Sit position, give the "Sit" command.
In training session, follow these stages:

• Put your dog on the lead.
• Stand in front of your dog.
• Hold the lead in your left hand, and have a tasty treat in your right hand.
• Show your dog the treat, and quickly close it in your hand.
• Move the treat towards your dog's nose, but fractionally higher (this action should push your dog's head up and backwards into his shoulders). As your dog follows the direction of the food, he will sit.
• Give the command "Sit" as your dog lowers his bottom into position.
• Immediately give the treat. Stroke and praise your dog in

An adult dog should respond to the verbal command instantly.

the Sit position, then release and play.
• Repeat the exercise.
• Practise the Sit response before feeding your dog and before you put him on the lead.

If your dog keeps jumping up or nudging for the treat, do not pull your hand away. This will only encourage him to follow your hand. Hold the treat very still in a closed hand, be patient, and only reward for sitting still.

The Down

Apply 'train as your dog does'. Any time your puppy naturally moves into the Down position, give the "Down" command. When training the Down, put your dog on the lead.

Use a treat to lure the dog into the Down.

• Your dog should be on your lefthand-side in the Sit position. Kneel beside your puppy.
• With the lead and a treat in your right hand, place the thumb and first finger of your left hand immediately behind the dog's shoulder blades.
• Using the treat, lure the dog's nose towards his chest, and then towards the ground at the point directly between his feet.
• In order to get the treat, the dog will begin to collapse. At this point, apply very light pressure behind the shoulder blades, (do not push, as this could cause resistance).
• As the dog moves into a Down position, slowly draw the treat forward and give the command "Down".
• Give the treat while gently stroking the dog with your left hand. Praise with a calm voice, give the release command and play.
• Repeat the exercise.

Apply light pressure on the shoulder blades to get the dog into the correct position.

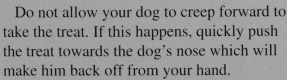

Do not allow your dog to creep forward to take the treat. If this happens, quickly push the treat towards the dog's nose which will make him back off from your hand.

Remember that misuse of commands will create a poor response e.g.:

"Sit down" – Which command do you mean, the Sit or the Down?

"Get down"– Some people instinctively use this command when the dog jumps up. Try to use a completely different command for jumping up at people or furniture, such as "Get off".

The Stay

The Stay command can be used in conjunction with the Sit, and the Down.

Stage One

• Once the dog is in the Sit or the Down position, use the "Stay" command. Count to five, then reward with a treat, release and play.

• Gradually increase the time of withholding the treat.

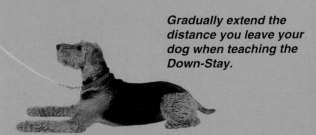

Gradually extend the distance you leave your dog when teaching the Down-Stay.

Second Stage

Now the handler must move position and gradually start to increase the distance between dog and handler.

Example I
- Put the dog in the Down position, kneel beside him and give the "Stay" command.
- Slowly stand up straight, repeating the "Stay" command. Hold the new position for a few seconds.
- Kneel down again by your dog's side, praise in position, reward, release and play.

Example II
- Put the dog in the Sit position, stand beside him and give the "Stay" command.
- Take one step to the right, repeating the "Stay" command. Hold the new position for a few seconds.
- Return to your dog's side, praise in position, reward, release and play.
- Stop using treats once you start to increase the distance of the Stay. The release and play should be sufficient reward if done enthusiastically.

The Sit-Stay: Remember to reward your dog when the exercise has been completed.

The Wait

This is a very useful command. Use it when you want your dog to remain stationary for a short time. It is best described as a temporary 'halt' before giving another command, e.g. when teaching recall or when opening a car or house door.

TRAINING TIP

At the completion of a successful exercise, reward your dog and praise him in that position, then give a 'release' command, such as "Finish" or "Okay".

19

Come

This is the most important and useful command you can ever teach your dog. When you first get your dog home, 'train as the dog does', as often as possible. Whenever the dog approaches you for attention or a cuddle, say: "Good girl/boy, come". Stroke him first, and then reward with a small treat.

Stage One

Formal early training for the Come command should always be carried out on a long line. This should measure 6-8ft in length.

• Hold the line and treat in your right hand, show the dog his treat and slowly back away.

• As the dog follows you, give the command "Come".

• Keep repeating the command over five to six paces. Then stroke the dog with your left hand, and give the treat. Give lots of verbal and physical praise.

• Keep the line short at this stage, as this will enable you to stop the puppy wandering off or avoiding interaction.

Stage One: Attach a training line and call the dog to you as you back off five or six paces.

Stage Two

Once a good response has been achieved in Stage One, you can progress to the next stage.

- With your puppy on your left, tell him to "Sit" and "Wait". Keep the line loose, and with a treat in the right hand, slowly turn and face your dog.
- Take one step backwards, stand still. Now call your dog's name and say "Come".
- Walk backwards as the dog approaches, reeling in the lead at the same time. Stroke and then give the treat. Reward with verbal and physical praise.
- Slowly increase the number of backward steps you take until you reach the end of the long line.

Stage Two: Tell the dog to "Wait", step back, gradually extending the distance, and call the dog in.

Stage Three

- With your dog on your left, tell him to "Sit" and "Wait", and calmly place the long line on the floor beside your dog.
- Turn and face your dog, repeat the "Wait" command, and back away a reasonable distance.
- Stand still (extend the time your puppy Sits and Waits gradually), call his name, give the command "Come", stroke and reward.

Stage Three: Lay the training line on the ground, face the dog, and then call him in.

On The Move

Practise these three stages in different locations so your dog learns that, as with all commands, they apply in all situations.

Introduce some distractions such as children playing or leaving a favourite toy nearby. Training classes will provide the opportunity to attempt the exercise when other dogs are around.

Reward intermittently to avoid complacency. You will achieve a more positive response if your dog does not know if he will receive a reward or not.

Your puppy is now ready to practise the "Come" response in a park or field. Choose a safe environment, a quiet time of day – and make sure your dog is hungry!

Stage Four

Free-run your puppy trailing the long line to enable you to reinforce the "Come" if response is poor. Once you are confident that you can achieve a good response from your puppy regularly, remove the long line to practise off-leash response.

Stage Four: Practise off-leash recalls.

Puppies often go through a 'deaf' stage around six months of age! If this happens, attach the long line again to remind your dog that you are still in control, even at a distance, and to re-establish the desired response.

The Retrieve

Most dogs enjoy retrieving – it is a useful game and it helps with recall training.

• Attach a favourite toy to a lightweight long line. Play with your dog to establish interest and enthusiasm in the toy.

First get your dog interested in the retrieve toy.

• Throw the toy a short distance, and allow your dog to chase after it and pick it up.

• Now call the dog to you, verbally praising as he approaches you. Do not make a grab for the toy.

• Physically praise your dog for at least thirty seconds before taking the toy away to throw it again.

The long line attached to the toy prevents the dog from running away with it.

Your dog should always enjoy coming back to you for that extra special praise you give before you take the toy away. If you fail to physically praise at this point, the dog will become reluctant to approach you holding the toy.

The dog runs out to get the toy – but the training line means the handler remains in control.

When your dog is returning the toy to you with enthusiasm, remove the long line.

New Challenges

Dog Training Classes

You can teach all the basic training exercises at home, but both you and your dog will benefit from attending dog training classes. However, finding a good dog training club is not always easy. Contact as many different sources for information as possible. Try your veterinary surgeon, pet shop, other dog owners, the local library or community information centre. Your national Kennel Club will provide a list of training clubs on request.

Before deciding on a suitable club, visit several, without taking your dog, and observe the methods of training. If you do not like the way things are done, try another club. Avoid those that advocate the use of punishment or excessive force.

Most clubs will take puppies as soon as they have completed their full course of

Dogs love agility, but you must be confident of having full control before attempting this discipline.

inoculations. Attending such classes should enable you to improve on responses and general behaviour. The instructor should teach you how to implement the basic commands and show you relevant handling techniques. Many clubs run the national Kennel Club's Good Citizen Scheme, which is a test of basic obedience for dog and handler.

Competitive Obedience requires accuracy, precision – and a lot of patience.

Specialised Training

If you want to improve your skills further, there are a variety of disciplines available, such as Competitive Obedience, Agility or Flyball, and your instructor should be able to advise you of a local club that specialises in the field you wish to pursue.

Troubleshooting

Despite all your efforts, sometimes problems occur in training. If these are dealt with effectively, at an early stage, undesirable behaviour can be corrected before the dog gets the upper hand in your relationship.

Problem 1: Jumping Up

My dog constantly jumps up at me, and at visitors when they first arrive in the house.

Jumping up can become a real problem.

Solutions

• Avoid touching the dog to push him off. Turn your back on him and do not make eye contact.
• Don't wait for your dog to jump up at you, counter command him to "Sit" as he approaches, and then praise him for doing so.
• Attach your dog to a long line. When you answer the door, allow the dog to go forward on a loose lead to greet the visitor. As soon as the dog attempts to jump up, take a step backwards and correct, saying "No". Then immediately allow your dog to go forward again. The dog will learn that he is allowed to go forward and greet, but on your terms. The visitor must not acknowledge the dog when he jumps up.
• Encourage visitors to ignore the dog for a few minutes and greet you first instead!

Keep your dog on a lead or a training line, and command him to "Sit" before he is greeted.

Problem 2: Poor Recall

My dog ignores me, or returns very slowly, when I ask him to "Come" at the end of a walk.

Solutions

It is the bad habits of the owner that are usually the cause for the breakdown in the "Come" response.

• Never tell your dog off for slow response to the "Come" command, however long you have waited. Praise when your dog returns – even through gritted teeth!

• Practise the "Come" response throughout the free run, so your dog never anticipates when he is going to be put back on the lead.

• Remember to use the word "Come". All too often, a handler calls the dog's name, but does not tell him what to do!

• Always reward your dog for returning to you, even if you have not called him.

Problem 3: Dog Aggression

My dog is aggressive towards other dogs that we meet when we are out on walks.

Solutions

• Allow plenty of early socialisation with other dogs as

Practise Recalls throughout a free run, so your dog does not anticipate the end of the walk – and the end of his freedom.

Troubleshooting

TRAINING TIP

If you plan to leave your dog on his own, or you want him to settle because you are expecting visitors, a short training session is more likely to achieve tiredness than a free run or a walk.

your dog grows up. Always praise good behaviour with other dogs.

• Protect your dog from obviously aggressive dogs. Avoid confrontation, cross the road, or change route in the park, if necessary.

• If your dog is growling at another dog, never stroke him or pick him up. This action will be perceived by your dog as praise of unacceptable behaviour. Ignore the behaviour and walk away and then call your dog to you. Do not start shouting and interfering. Most dogs will sort out their differences more quickly and more easily if you don't get involved.

• If you meet another dog when your dog is on the lead, use the "Come" command to encourage your dog to walk on. Once he has greeted the dog, try to keep the lead slack, then call his name and command "Come". Reward your dog with an irresistible treat once he has walked away and acknowledged you.

Dogs that are used to socialising from an early age will rarely become aggressive with other dogs.

Problem 4: The Worried Dog

My dog seems worried when strangers come to the house.

Solutions

•Do not coax your dog to greet strangers. Avoid using praise, such as "Good girl", to encourage a more confident attitude – all you will be doing is praising shyness. Ignore the behaviour and concentrate on the visitor.

• Encourage visitors to ignore the dog. They should not make eye contact with the dog, talk to him or try to touch him. Most importantly, do not allow visitors to pursue the dog.

• Before you answer the door, attach your dog to a long line. This will increase his level of confidence. Ask your dog to Sit, and do not force him forward to greet visitors. Control any barking with a sharp "No". Once the visitors are in the house, allow the dog to trail the line and move around freely. If the dog approaches a visitor, he should

Do not force a worried dog to greet visitors.

Wait until the dog is ready to make an approach, and reward with a treat.

TRAINING TIP

To deter your puppy from chewing anything made of wood, apply a liberal coating of washing - up liquid to the chewed area. Do not use mustard, chilli, or tabasco as dogs love these hot spicy flavours.

be ignored. Once the dog has voluntarily approached the visitor two or three times, the visitor should offer a tasty treat. Reward the dog for approaching, not for backing off or running away.

• The dog will quickly gain confidence if the visitor avoids eye contact and resists trying to touch the dog.

Problem 5: Destructive Behaviour

My dog is very destructive, particularly when he is left on his own.

Solutions

• Ensure you dog is mentally tired before leaving it. A short training session will achieve this.

• Leave your dog with something to do. A nylon bone will keep him occupied.

• Give him an old item of your clothing. This will act as a comforter in your absence.

• Practise leaving your dog for short periods – five minutes at a time to start with. Gradually increase

Destructive behaviour can be caused by boredom or by anxiety.

the period of time he is left alone. Remember to reward good behaviour.

• Try to make your departures and arrivals as non-eventful as possible. Don't make a big issue of going out.

• Unless you catch your dog in the act of chewing, never scold him on your return. You might think he knows what he has done because he is cringing in the corner, but, in fact, he is only responding to your body language and cross voice.

• Invest in an indoor crate. These are very good for teaching your dog to settle while you are out. Your dog may be in need of a more secure resting place, and the correct use an indoor crate can provide this.

Finally, remember that it is your responsibility to give your dog the confidence and training to behave in an acceptable manner. 99% of dogs are eager to please; 99% of owners will end up with the dog they deserve!

Try to make departures and arrivals non-eventful so your dog does not become worried.